Duckling Duckling

Edited by Linda Meyer and Fiona Tang

Paperback ISBN: 978-1-943241-00-2
EPUB ISBN: 978-1-943241-05-7
Mobipocket ISBN: 978-1-943241-20-0
ePDF ISBN: 978-1-943241-25-5

Library of Congress Control Number: 2015937910

Phonic Monic Books
www.phonicmonic.com

C&C Joint Printing Co. (Guangdong) Ltd.
Chunhu Industrial Eatate, Pinghu
Long Gang, Shenzhen, PRC 518111
www.candcprinting.com

First Edition – April 2016

Image Credits:
Cover pg. Anneka/Shutterstock, Editor pg. Africa Studio/Shutterstock, Dedication pg. Sevenke/Shutterstock, Anneka/Shutterstock; 1, Tsekhmister/Shutterstock; 2, Volodymyr Goinyk/Shutterstock; 3, Volodymyr Goinyk/Shutterstock; 4, Volodymyr Goinyk/Shutterstock; 5, Anneka/Shutterstock; 6, Africa Studio/Shutterstock; 7, Dennis Tabler/Shutterstock; 8, Africa Studio/Shutterstock; 9, Volodymyr Goinyk/Shutterstock; 10, Africa Studio/Shutterstock; 11, Africa Studio/Shutterstock; 12, Paul Reeves Photography/Shutterstock; 13, Stargazer//Shutterstock; 14, Anneka/Shutterstock; 15, Africa Studio/Shutterstock; 16, Gleb Semenjuk/Shutterstock; 17, Photo House/Shutterstock; 18, Otmar Smit/Shutterstock; 19, aabeele/Shutterstock; 20, Tomatito/Shutterstock; 21, Steve Oehlenschlager/Shutterstock; 22, Stargazer/Shutterstock; 23, Eric Isselee/Shutterstock; 24, Coffeemill/Shutterstock ; 25, Robert Eastman/Shutterstock; 26, Gary Stone/Shutterstock; 27, AE Photographic/Shutterstock; 28, stockoftor/Shutterstock; 29, Anneka/Shutterstock; 30, Anneka/Shutterstock; 31, Africa Studio/Shutterstock; 33.

This book is dedicated to my husband and children.
You are my inspiration!

Duckling, duckling,

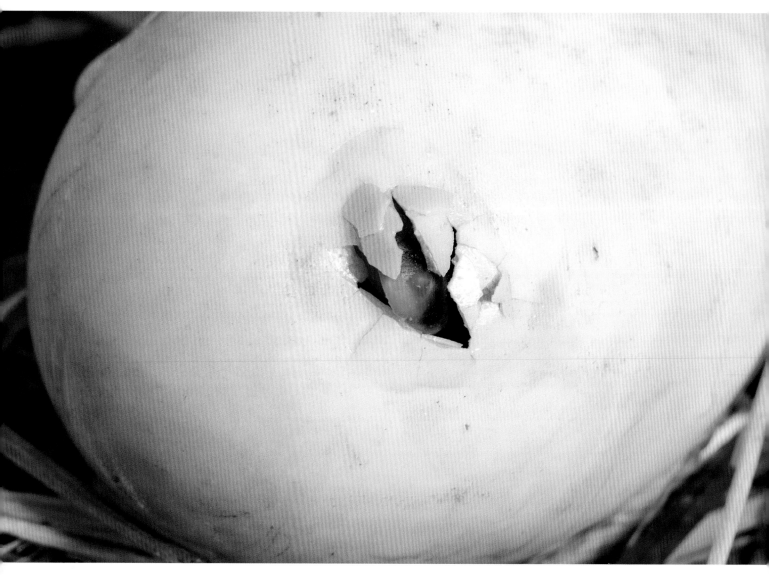

Egg goes crack.

Duckling, duckling,

You can hatch.

Duckling, duckling,

In the meadow.

Duckling, duckling,

Sweet and yellow.

Duckling, duckling,

Bill so neat.

Duckling, duckling,

Nice webbed feet.

Duckling, duckling,

Feathers so fine.

Duckling, duckling,

Waddle in a line.

Duckling, duckling,

On the ground.

Duckling, duckling,

Squeaking sounds.

Duckling, duckling,

Eat your lunch.

Duckling, duckling,

Munch, munch, munch.

Duckling, duckling,

In the pond.

Duckling, duckling,

Family bond.

Duckling, duckling,

Nice fine weather.

Duckling, duckling,

Grow your feathers.

Duckling, duckling,

Look at you now!

You're a big duck!

Wow!

Quacking duck, quacking duck,

Do your thing.

Quacking duck, quacking duck,

Flap your wings.

Quacking duck, quacking duck,

Fly here and there.

Quacking duck, quacking duck,

Fly everywhere.

Quacking duck, quacking duck,

Swim around.

Quacking duck, quacking duck,

Make quacking sounds.

Quacking duck, quacking duck,

Eat your snacks.

Quacking duck, quacking duck,

Quack, quack, quack!

Quacking duck, quacking duck,

Do your best.

Quacking duck, quacking duck,

Build your nest.

Quacking duck, quacking duck,

Lay eggs in a batch.

One day, one day,

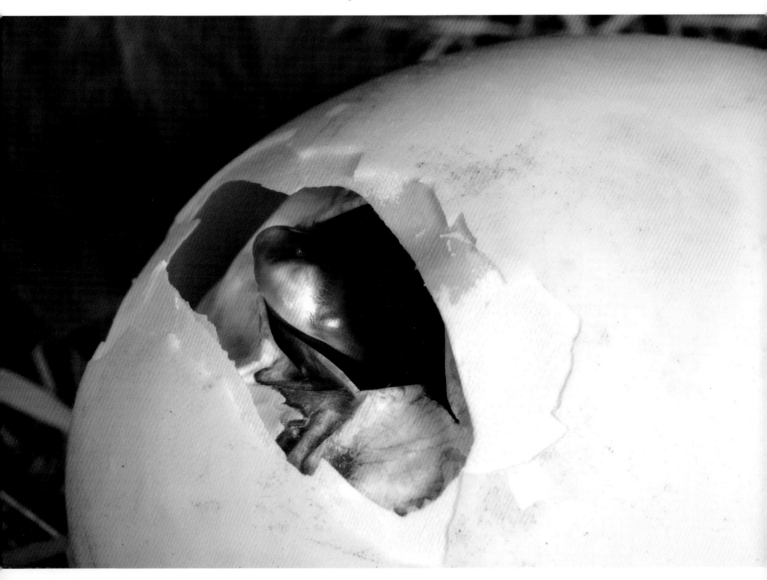

Eggs will hatch.

About the Author

Cammie Ho lives with her husband and two children in California, where she studied and obtained her Elementary School Teaching Credential and her Master's Degree in Teaching English as a Second Language.

Cammie loves reading books to her children, and is inspired by her favorite children's book authors, Dr. Seuss and Bill Martin Jr. She is developing an early learning program using music and chants to teach young children, believing that children learn well through a variety of fun channels. She writes lyrics and produces songs that teach reading and spelling in a program called Phonic Monic.

www.phonicmonic.com